AF264403

# My Journey with MS:
## A Story of Change, Hope, Faith, and Resilience

### Kimberly Pettus

Bolden Fields Publishing/Bolden Fields, LLC Bowie, MD 20715

www.boldenfieldspublishing.com



Editor's Note:
This publication is not intended as a substitute for the advice of healthcare professionals.

Final interior design and typesetting by Bolden Fields Publishing, LLC

# DEDICATION

*I want to dedicate this book specifically to Terence, my husband; Rene, my sister; my children; and my friends, as they have provided transportation and support. Without them, I would not have made it during this unexpected challenge!*

# Contents

# *Chapter 1: Notes and Apps*

"I feel like every day, I'm supposed to be doing something." I realize that this feeling comes up when I am anxious because I have not met some goal. The truth is, I don't move like I used to move, and I don't remember like I used to remember. Deep down, I just feel like I need to achieve something.

My husband always asks me, "Why do you think that?" as if to say, "What makes you think you have not achieved something?" or "What makes you think that you need to be doing something other than what you're already doing?" He's right, of course; I have achieved much in this life. From earning a bachelor's degree in finance and accounting and a master's in business management to becoming a CPA while raising a family, I have done quite a bit. Yet I am also here now, living, and I want to do more.

The truth is, I have multiple sclerosis (MS). MS is what it is each day, and every day can be totally different. I never know if I am going to have a good day or a bad day until I experience it. In this process, I've had to go back to reminding myself of who I am, what I'm good at, and what is it I can do in that moment and just do that. Constantly reminding myself of these truths has become essential on my journey.

At the beginning, I learned from my family members that I was not always doing the things that I needed to do. I was also extremely tired. I understood that I had to ask for help and ask for what I needed.

When I went to the physical therapist, she gave me a whole list of exercises and activities that I needed to do to maintain my strength. I had pictures to show me what I needed to do, and I had it in my mind that I needed to break a sweat doing these exercises. (That is *not* what physical therapy is.) I used to get frustrated, as I felt like I wasn't doing anything, so I started to do the exercises how I wanted and decided I wasn't going to do as many reps as the therapist suggested. So, I would do them the right way one time and then maybe do them once more my way another time. Then I started not doing the exercises at all. (Yes, doing it my way can become a slippery slope.)

Instead, I would sit in front of the TV doing nothing—sitting all day and not getting up and moving. Then I found myself hurting. My legs started to hurt and weren't able to be as flexible as they should have been, which forced me to get up and stand throughout the day and walk around a bit. The Apple watch my sister gave me helped me to keep track of how long I had been sitting as well. This is when I realized that I was not getting stronger and my balance was not getting better.

The other part of this is that my husband called me out for not doing my exercises. Yes, he sure did! I was not the most appreciative of him doing this at first, yet I knew he was right; I had to change. I had to shift my perspective. I had to stop thinking I knew everything, follow what the professionals told me, and do the exercises I was supposed to do. Now, I take breaks from sitting and will go and do my leg lifts as a part of my routine, and it helps!

Going to the physical therapist activated the beginning of a transformative phase for me—a journey filled with newly created habits that helped me to succeed.

I figured out at that moment that I needed to embrace using notes, apps, and even sticky notes.

Embracing notes and apps as reminders proved to be instrumental. By embracing these tools, I was able to write down my deadlines, track my necessary tasks, and get things done. There are so many tools and options available to help me keep track of things, but among the countless options, an app called <u>Todoist</u>[1] stood out as my most trusted ally.

You see, <u>Todoist</u> offers me the perfect platform to record my deadlines and essential tasks, ensuring I never miss a beat. The best part is that it syncs to my email, providing me with an easy-to-access list of all the things that need my attention: people to call, tasks to tackle, and everything in between.

Of course, we all have our preferences, and yours might differ from mine. The key lesson here is to find the tool that resonates with you and complements your unique style. For me, physical sticky notes were a popular choice at first, scattered strategically throughout my surroundings.

---

[1] I am an affiliate for Todoist. This means I make income from any sales made through the link provided in the above text in relation to Todoist. Link: https://get.todoist.io/76a5msjc54fn

However, I learned the hard way that their downside lies in the risk of misplacement—truly a reminder that even reminders require some safeguarding. Make sure that you notate whatever you needed a note about electronically or some way that you can go back to it if it's lost. After all, the point is to be able to remember.

Once I got organized, balance, both physically and mentally, became my next focus. Balance was something I used to take for granted before MS came into my life. Simple actions like maintaining proper posture, rolling my shoulders back and down, or taking larger steps while still maintaining my balance took on a whole new significance. Doing those things might seem like a no-brainer to someone without MS, but it is different for me, and I soon realized that I needed reminders to build up my balance as well.

We don't think about how often we keep our balance and keep ourselves from falling daily. You typically don't just fall over—or if you do, it's usually not a problem—but with MS, it becomes a big problem. So, I had to go back to the fundamentals. I was revisiting the basics, just as one learns to walk during infancy. My trusty apps and notes became my personal assistants, prompting me to mindfully practice these fundamental tasks and thus prevent accidents.

I had to be sure that I was doing what I could, because there were so many things that I had no control over. I couldn't control the fact that I had MS. I couldn't control the fact that I needed help. And so, I took on the mindset of needing to control what I could. Even though I was hesitant, I started carrying my cane with me and began to realize that I truly did need it. If I didn't have it, I could fall. I then carried my cane everywhere, and I had a note to remind me about that as well!

Acceptance played a significant role in my growth. Initially, I hesitated to embrace mobility aids like my cane or a walker, and certainly not my wheelchair. The idea of needing such assistance felt like admitting defeat. But soon, I realized that controlling what I could was essential. Carrying my cane became second nature, a symbol of my realization of the support I needed. This was key for me, as I had to actually *use* these items versus just having them at home, still being in denial and facing accidents along the way. One of the things I was very prideful about at the beginning of my diagnosis was that I didn't want to use my cane. I didn't want to use my walker. I didn't want to use my wheelchair. To sum it all up, I didn't want to have MS at all.

Eventually, I wholeheartedly accepted and utilized every available tool — my walker, my cane, *and* my wheelchair — as I learned that there's no shame in seeking support when needed.

Navigating daily life with MS also brought with it its share of curious remarks from well-intentioned folks. Some would express their surprise, stating, "You don't *look* like you have MS." I thought, "Well, what does MS look like?"

Though their words grated on my nerves, I learned to rise above it, reminding myself that their comments arose from a place of misunderstanding. And for those of you reading my story, if somebody tells you they have MS, please don't make that statement too many people have said to me! Just inquire about how they are doing or how they're feeling today instead of using condescending or dismissive words.

There is something about human beings where in our mind, we think we *have* to say something, and so people will say whatever pops into their head. We have to remember that we do not always have to have something to say.

Education then became my mission, and I patiently answered questions, debunking misconceptions along the way. I also eventually got to the point where I had to just learn to control myself. I chose not to get upset, because getting upset doesn't bode well for me; it causes me to not be able to maintain my balance and do what I need to do. I started just letting it go, or letting it roll like water off of a duck's back. I would just let it roll off and move on to the next thing.

My growth demanded resilience. Letting go of offense and choosing not to dwell on insensitive remarks became my armor against negativity. Instead of dwelling on the past, I embraced a forward-looking approach, staying focused on the next challenge that lay ahead. Positivity and proactivity propelled me forward on my path of learning and self-improvement.

Taking charge of my health meant learning as much as I could about MS and the resources available. I started researching and gathering information that would support my improved health journey.

I also confronted my tiredness. The challenges of MS often made me feel like an airplane without enough fuel to take off or like the "game over" sound in a video game when you run out of lives.

I had to be mindful of the language I used and the thoughts I entertained. Saying "I am tired" perpetuated the feeling of exhaustion. Instead, I needed to focus on how to address and overcome the feeling of tiredness. Prioritizing a good night's sleep and making positive choices helped me wake up with more energy and readiness to face the day.

Part of my process was choosing to take charge of my health every single day. For example, there are times when I am by myself and have to prepare my own meals. I can choose to prepare something that is going to benefit me — like meals containing fruits, vegetables, or a source of protein — or I can choose to snack on cookies. I have to remember what I want in this whole process, and what I want is to maintain my balance. Having cookies and sugary stuff around is fine, and having a bit of it here and there is okay for some people. Yet if all I eat is sugar, that will not help me to maintain balance or good nutrition. I have to keep all of this in perspective when I make my decisions each day.

Armed with knowledge, I sought out assistance and implemented newfound information into my daily life. Sometimes I'd battle against a specific area of resistance, such as my dislike for exercise. However, I soon discovered the benefits of exercise, particularly in managing my energy, having more energy overall, and maintaining my balance. The truth is that previously, it was hard for me to exercise because I had never liked working out anyway.

When I used to work out before MS, I wasn't one of those people who went to the gym, worked out, liked the results, and felt that was enough. After working out, if someone asked me, "How do you feel?" I would say, "I feel great." Ha! No, I did not feel great—I hated it every step of the way, and it's no different now. Nothing changes with MS in that manner. I just try not to have an opinion about it and focus on doing what I know I need to do. Exercising also helps me use up my energy and tire myself out so I can fall asleep better at night. So, even though exercising still feels like a challenge, I am resolved to do what is necessary for my well-being.

I'm constantly learning, and once I've learned something, I try to incorporate it into my life and keep myself accountable. That is what I've been doing, and if I'm honest, it's a full-time job. Sometimes I'm in constant pain and just want to go to bed, but then I feel like I have to be doing something. The bigger truth is that my biggest enemy is me. But with God on my side, even I can't stop me.

Life with MS has uncovered profound lessons. It has taught me to know and embrace myself fully, to appreciate the strengths that I possess, and to keep moving forward with determination and grace. And so, my journey continues—one of growth, understanding, and the pursuit of a life lived to the fullest.

# Chapter 2: Embracing Change and Adapting to the Journey

"My biggest enemy is me. And even I can't stop me." — Andy Mineo

When I was first diagnosed, I did not maintain good habits for living with MS. I would try to eat everything that I used to eat before my diagnosis, especially unhealthy food and candy (sugar). If you know anything about MS, then you know that diet is incredibly important.

I was eating sugar fairly often, as my children would get me whatever I asked for. But then my husband recruited them to be the keepers of my health, so they stopped sneaking me sugar, and now they don't enable my wrongdoing anymore. Ha! In all seriousness, sugar is really not my friend. Thus, I had to begin forming healthy habits so I could keep my balance in check and function at my best.

As I sought guidance from a physical therapist—and having my husband get the children on the same side as him, as they were all in cahoots to be sure not to cave into my requests—I began building habits that would pave the way to my success. Keeping track of tasks and appointments became a lifeline and allowed me to research foods that would be helpful for me in navigating life with MS.

They knew that it was a part of my diagnosis and understood that I was not trying to be a certain way or express an unpleasant attitude on purpose. MS impacts my brain in a way that I often forget things, so yes, having my short-term memory not be what it used to, I was frustrated. I didn't understand this, though, in the moments it was happening, nor did I expect my life to be impacted in this way.

My diagnosis changed my family in many ways. My family had to change the way they engaged with me and provide more care while also modeling for me ways that I could be patient with myself along this journey. In doing so, our roles shifted. My daughter was caring for me in ways that most mothers care for their children, keeping the house and, when she got old enough, driving me places. My son was deeply impacted by my diagnosis, as he had to do more things around the house and provide more care for me as well. My children ended up doing the things for me that I used to be able to do for them.

Initially, I didn't think much about my attitude, especially when my doctor asked me about it during my visits to the MS clinic. I always brushed it off, but deep down, I was angry. At times, I was angry at God. When I felt out of control and that I just wanted to hit someone, I was reminded of James Weldon Johnson's phrase he used in his novel *The Autobiography of an Ex-Colored Man*: "Your arms are too short to box with God." At that moment I realized that God is in control, and if I was trying to fight him to have my way, I wouldn't win. I had to take a moment to slow down my thoughts and recognize how absurd they

Now, I eat a lot of greens and fruit, especially if I have a craving for sugar. In the past, I tried the Wahls Protocol[2] where you have to eat six cups of greens every day with your diet. I would have spinach, kale, and other greens every day, and in the mornings I'd have eggs and plums and things of this nature as well.

Eating healthy has greatly helped with my moods and brain fog. "Although it was difficult at first to make these changes, I had to do what helped me and what made me feel my best." When I was eating all of that sugar and candy, I was *not* feeling my best. I didn't feel like I could run a marathon, so I had to shift my habits and stick to my new way of eating. (Being able to run a marathon should be how everyone feels, right!?) This is the wisdom I came to that supports me in feeling my best and helps my progress come more easily.

However, my thoughts have not always worked in my favor . . . I have thoughts that wander where they want to go. There are times when I go down the rabbit hole and don't come back. I have to ask myself, "What are we doing, Kim?" to bring myself back to the present. I have to encourage myself to keep going and keep moving forward. Many times, we will face unwanted, unforeseen change and transition—we all do in life—just as I have with being diagnosed with MS. What I know is that when I start to feel

---

[2] Wahls, Terry L and Eve. Adamson. 2014. The Wahls Protocol: A Radical New Way to Treat All Chronic Autoimmune Conditions Using Paleo Principles. Penguin Group USA.

hopeless, I can encourage myself to keep enjoying life, keep doing things that I love, or find new hobbies to engage with.

There are so many things in life that can be distracting to me now as well, but I get to choose what I want to focus on. My goal is to choose to not become distracted. For example, I had one person compliment me recently, and the response that came up in my mind was "If you really knew." I had to realize that sometimes thoughts will come up, and I have to challenge them and say, "That's not true," and see what *is* true for me instead. Then I challenge myself to think through my life and see who I am and what I have accomplished. I have been through a whole lot in life. I am still here, and I can keep moving forward.

I went through all of that to be here now. This whole journey has brought me to where I am today. I took time to study and get all kinds of degrees, and I can come down on myself pretty tough when I feel like I am not living up to certain standards. I will think to myself, "Kim, what are you doing here? You are not doing anything that is going to help you." These are the times when I'm not having a good MS day and start to become very critical, telling myself that I'm not doing what I should be doing.

For instance, one day I was watching TV. I was enjoying what I was watching, and then suddenly I thought, "I've spent way too much time watching TV. I am not doing what I'm supposed to be doing." I had to encourage myself to get up and move and go do something. Though I do believe in sometimes just taking time to enjoy a moment, I realized that I had been in this particular moment for a *long* time. So, I decided to go and get dressed, look at my phone, see what my next daily task was, and see what I had accomplished that day. Had I truly been staring at the TV all day, or had I gotten something done? This keeps me honest.

Of course, there are also times when I see that spending time talking with someone *is* the right thing to do at the moment. For example, if I'm conversing with someone and helping them to feel better, I check in with myself. I check the time and tell myself, "This is actually not taking up that much time." I then decide to give myself a half hour to be in the moment, and after the half hour, I will wrap up the conversation and move on to the next thing.

Perhaps most importantly, I've learned that if I am going to be a critic, I can also be a cheerleader. I take whatever I face in my life and turn it into something I can use. In fact, that is how my book came about. It is taking my story and sharing it with others. It is using my skill sets to help someone else along their journey. It is me being me, facing challenges, overcoming those challenges, and moving forward in ways that best support my journey. It is always remembering that I've been through challenges before. Any new challenge is the same thing — it may have a different face or a different name, but I've done it before, and yes, I can journey through it again. I know me, and I know how to encourage myself.

Growing up, I had always thought I was going to be one thing as far as my career was concerned, yet when I got there, it was not what I thought it was. So, my next thought was, "Well, what are you going to do now?" I knew I needed to shift, and I knew that I could make that shift and encourage myself to do that.

Initially on this journey, there was one person in my life who would say to me, "Well you can't do that" or "What are you going to do about that?" One, yes, I don't have them in my life any longer, and two, I learned in the process of dealing with that person that I know myself. I know who I am, and I know what I can do and what I have done. Now with MS, it is not the same way that I have always done things, yet there is always another way; I just have to be willing to do it and figure it out.

I even heard from one of my doctors, "You know that MS can't be cured." All that makes anyone want to do is just go lie down and not do anything! But the truth is that you can do many things to help your symptoms and to feel better.

Even going on this journey of writing this book has been very therapeutic for me, as in the process I was able to look over my journey and see all the progress I've made. Others can only encourage you based on their own experiences, what you may have told them, or what they think they know about you, so it is important to be able to encourage yourself, as you are the one who knows you best.

The Cosby Kids used to say that "every hero needs a soundtrack."[3] So, one thing I use to encourage myself is a playlist I listen to regularly that contains everything from

---

[3] Cosby, William H. (1972-1984). *Fat Albert and the Cosby Kids – The Original Animated Series.* Entertainment Rights PLC.

gospel music to music from *Rocky* to whatever it is that inspires me.

I also start each day with a Bible verse. I actually have an app that sends me a Bible verse every day, so every morning I read my daily verse and then go to my encouraging playlist, put it on shuffle, and listen to four songs. Listening to songs from my playlist helps to shift my mood, especially if I am in a lot of pain.

It also helps me to set goals in terms of the time I want to spend on something. My sleep is the biggest thing that has shifted for me. There are times when I want to sleep and can't, and other times when I need to sleep but don't want to. My motivational items and habits are really helpful when I am lying in bed awake, feeling like I can't get up or do something.

The truth is that I am walking this journey and helping myself through the diagnosis, and many people can learn from the things you need to do to mitigate symptoms, stay motivated, and live your life in the present. There is hope in living with MS. All the things you do, you do them to have a better quality of life. There is so much opportunity to engage in the negativity from people outside of this experience. Instead, why not go within and engage your creativity, your positivity? Why not begin to live in that place and live it loudly?

# *Chapter 3: Navigating Mood Swings and Embracing Adaptation*

Whenever my doctor asked me how I was doing, I would say, "I'm fine." However, I later learned I was not fine.

There was something much deeper going on beneath the surface. Soon, it became clear I could no longer perform the role that I had spent hours being trained to do at work. I had a whole lot of knowledge but an inability to execute, and I felt horrible, frustrated, and confused. I was known for being efficient and I could always type quickly, but one day I woke up and had no feeling on my entire left side. I felt like, "Oh, wow, that's one more thing." I did not know what was going on; I thought it was a new symptom of carpal tunnel.

I had to work that day, but I couldn't type as I did before. I had no feeling in my arm at all, and I could no longer type without looking at the keyboard. As time went on, I realized I could no longer type as fast as I used to. Since my job required typing, I was not sure what I would be able to do.

This experience felt so unfair. I had no one to blame, yet I wanted to hit someone. I felt out of control—I was losing my ability to type. Worse still, no one could explain what was happening to me in the beginning.

Honestly, I didn't know what I didn't know. I believed I had carpal tunnel, and that stuck in my mind even when one doctor mentioned he suspected MS; I was not mentally in the place to explore that possibility initially. If I would've paid more attention, I would've known.

I changed doctors due to insurance and ended up having surgery to correct my "carpal tunnel," as I had told my doctors that this was the issue that needed attending to. After the surgery, they did a conduction study where they put a charge into my body to see if it was conducting properly and if I could feel anything. What I didn't know then that I know now is that, of course, I would fail that test.

It came back that I did not have any feeling in that wrist. This is a function of MS, not carpal tunnel; if it was carpal tunnel, I would have had feeling after surgery. This was when the doctors went down the road of figuring out what was really going on with me. I had many other procedures done, including a spinal tap, where they take fluid out of your spinal cord to test for MS, and an MRI for them to see what was going on in my brain. When they did the MRI, they could see that I had lesions on my spinal cord leading to my brain, and that is when they diagnosed me with MS. This entire process took about a year and a half.

On top of all of this, my job wanted me to come up with accommodations for the work I was doing based on my diagnosis, which is so ironic and funny. Nobody knows how MS will or won't develop and what accommodations one will need. You never know what will happen in the future with MS; it is different for every person, as there are different impacts on the body depending on where the lesions are on your brain. MS is a cognitive disease, and it is such a giant miscellaneous illness. Some people have been studying MS for years and still don't understand how it will impact an individual.

Living with MS has caused me to experience many different things. One new experience was that I went through crazy swings in my emotions. Some days I felt fine, and the next day everything felt off. Initially, I didn't see the effects of my mood swings. It was only in my interactions with my husband that I truly saw the impact of my moods on my family.

Honestly, I believed I was fine at first and that my attitude was unchanged, but talking to my family made me realize otherwise. They pointed out how my attitude had shifted during one of my podcast recordings.

To truly understand what was happening, I decided to conduct a "family and friends" episode where I interviewed my loved ones, including my husband. During that conversation, the truth hit me like an epiphany. They weren't being mean or unfair; they were simply stating the truth—I wasn't the same as before. I had to acknowledge that my mood was indeed fluctuating, likely due to the one thing that people with MS commonly experience: emotional swings.

My family told me about their experiences with me and how they had to be more patient, as I was not currently able to do what I thought I could do—they knew that, yet I did not. I couldn't see it at the time. There were even times when they felt that they had to "pardon" my behavior! My attitude had impacted them in ways that I can only imagine now, but the other side of this is that they showed me grace.

were. Why would I fight the one who is always there for me and looking out for my own good? I just had to stay in it long enough to see the end, despite my physical pain, cognitive impairment, anger, and frustration.

At the time that I was going through these feelings, I was in a very timely study of Habakkuk. I understood Habakkuk's frustration when he cried out to God, wondering why all this bad stuff was happening and why God had not stopped it. Habakkuk, like me, came to understand who God is and that God was sovereign and could be trusted. I just had to stop going that deep and do my part.

So, I decided to talk to my physical therapist and doctor about the impact of my attitude on my progress in physical therapy and overall health. Through several therapy sessions and conversations with my doctors, I learned that my attitude actually played a significant role in my progress. It wasn't just about doing the exercises as prescribed; it was also about maintaining a positive mindset and staying committed to my goals.

With the support of my tribe and my sister, I also started incorporating exercise into my routine by following the MS Gym and watching online videos. My sister, despite living miles away, motivated me through Zoom workouts, and I began to see the impact of my workouts on my attitude. It helped me progress both physically and mentally.

I had to come to terms with my feelings and accept that they were valid, but I also had to decide what I wanted for my life. MS had disrupted my plans and affected my work, but I couldn't let it defeat me. I had to adapt and find solutions, such as going through occupational therapy to regain the ability to use my hands effectively for typing. It was a humbling experience, accepting that I needed help and making the necessary adjustments to reach my goals, but I was also learning how best to apply therapy and do my part.

The cognitive impact of MS was something I hadn't anticipated. It affected my work and my interactions with others, and I had to be mindful of my diet, exercise, and sleep to maintain a positive attitude and manage my cognitive struggles. I wouldn't let myself spiral into frustration; instead, I relied on my family and my faith in God, knowing that He was with me on this journey.

My journey with MS has taught me that there is no one-size-fits-all approach. Each person's experience with MS is unique, and I had to find what worked best for me. While it was challenging to deal with the unpredictability that MS brings, I have learned to stay in the present and take things one step at a time. I couldn't control everything, even though I wanted to . . . but I could control my attitude and approach to the challenges I faced.

Though it felt like my previous plans had been shattered, I learned to write a new script for my life, focusing on what I *could* do rather than dwelling on what I couldn't. I had to let go of my pride, accept help, and utilize the support of my husband, children, sister, health professionals, and other supportive people in my life. Together, we found solutions that accommodated my needs, allowing me to continue working and maintaining a fulfilling life.

In the face of MS, I discovered strength I didn't know I had—strength that came from relying on God and my incredible support system. This journey has been far from easy, but I keep moving forward, recognizing that the path to progress isn't linear but rather filled with twists and turns. I may not have all the answers or know what lies ahead, but with God, determination, and the right attitude, I continue to navigate my life with MS, ready to face whatever comes my way.

# *Chapter 4: Gaining Balance with Prism Glasses*

At first glance, they might look like regular glasses, but their magic lies in their ability to deflect light and properly align images, correcting visual issues associated with MS. These prism glasses—those special little spectacles that help alleviate some MS symptoms—became my next adventure.

I decided to visit an ophthalmologist who specializes in MS to explore the possibility of getting some of these glasses. Initially, I didn't really think I needed new glasses, but as they say, you don't know what you don't know. As I went through the fitting process, trying on different glasses with various prism strengths, I walked down the hallway trying to gauge how they affected my balance. The earlier ones felt like I was on a ship at sea, swaying back and forth, but as we kept adjusting the prism strength, I finally found the one that made me feel stable and grounded.

It was fascinating how these seemingly ordinary glasses could have such a significant impact on me. The proper prism strength made a world of difference in how I felt while walking. It was like a revelation—something as simple as glasses could improve my stability and overall experience with MS!

Being more than twenty years old, I needed bifocals, but more specifically I needed lined bifocals to help my mind know where the middle of my sight was and maintain a frame of reference.

My husband was with me and gave his much-needed input on the style, helping me find the frames that fit my style and face best. With his and the technician's help, I chose my frames and ordered two pairs of prism glasses. I joked with my husband about how these lined bifocals might not be the sexiest choice, but if they worked, I was all for it.

And thus began the waiting game. Waiting for the glasses to be ready was a test of patience, but once they arrived, I was eager to put them on and see how they transformed my daily life—and they did not disappoint. Life took on a new sense of balance, and I felt more in control of my movements. The difference was a total game-changer.

But of course, nothing good comes without a price. The glasses were quite expensive—over $400. My husband and I had to discuss how and when we would be able to afford them, as we had to pay upfront before the order could be completed. It was a considerable expense, but when it came to improving my well-being, I knew it was a necessary investment.

Even though at first I thought that the price might be on the higher side, upon further research I realized that the cost was competitive, considering the range of prism glasses could go up to $1,500 and beyond. And the glasses themselves were just the beginning; additional features could be added as well depending on personal preferences and individual needs.

This experience taught me a valuable lesson: improving your quality of life is always worth the investment. I hadn't known that my balance could be significantly affected by how I see things until my vision was corrected by these glasses.

MS can be a tricky condition, and sometimes the solutions are unexpected. Once I became aware of the correctable issue, I knew it was up to me to figure it out and keep moving forward.

The journey with MS is full of surprises, and these prism glasses were just another example of how finding the right tools could significantly improve my quality of life. I was grateful for the specialized care from the ophthalmologist and the lab lady who helped me find the perfect fit.

So, with my new glasses on, I embraced the world with a newfound sense of stability, ready to face whatever else MS had in store for me. With each step, I continue to learn more about myself and my diagnosis and gain strength and understanding that helps me navigate the unpredictable terrain of multiple sclerosis.

# *Chapter 5: Being Let Go and Letting Go*

Living with MS is like being on a rollercoaster of emotions. One day I would feel fine, and the next I was struggling. My MRI results also confirmed the lesions on my brain and spinal cord, providing clarity about the physical and cognitive challenges I faced. It was frustrating to realize that my job would continue to be affected by my declining typing ability and cognitive impairments.

I was let go from a number of different jobs, as I was no longer able to sustain a specific output of work in the time frame my supervisors wanted or that the job required for its employees. I quickly learned that I could not focus on what I was not able to do or was newly incapable of doing. Instead, I decided to focus on what I *could* do and seek ways to make adjustments and accommodations that worked for me.

Work need not be my focus.

The question that was important for me to answer was:

Can I make it and figure it out, even with MS?

And that is how I ended up writing this book and creating an opportunity for me to share my story with others. The deep truth is that everyone's journey with MS is different, and there are no easy answers or solutions when faced with this diagnosis. You have to find ways to create new neural pathways in your mind to compensate for the loss of functions, even without medical intervention. The human body is adaptable, and this is how I know that a MS diagnosis can be managed.

You have to realize the way that your body and mind work on any given day, be kind to yourself, and move forward on your journey with that. Every day is a new experience for everyone, and with MS, you will experience new challenges with your cognition and physically navigating the world. It is all about how you process what you are going through and how you work to adapt to the new challenges you may be facing.

The journey with MS is full of ups and downs, but I always persevered, focusing on what I could do and finding strength in my support system. With each step, I learned more about myself and my capabilities. MS might have changed the course of my life, but it will not break my spirit. I am determined to keep moving forward, relying on the love and encouragement of my family and friends and, most importantly, trusting in God's plan for me.

# Chapter 6 - The Power of Support Groups

As I navigated the trials of living with MS, I discovered the value of having experts and support groups by my side. Support groups provided me with a wealth of knowledge and wisdom as others shared similar experiences to my own, and listening to speakers who attended these groups opened my eyes to new perspectives and insights.

A social worker from my healthcare company once stressed the importance of surrounding myself with people who are also facing chronic illnesses as a way of support. Sharing experiences and finding common ground with one's struggles provides a sense of normalizing what you are going through. Knowing that others are experiencing what you are experiencing — and that you are not crazy! — is deeply comforting. It is a relief to know that you're not alone on your journey.

I have tried various methods of attending support groups or group therapy, from using online platforms to attending in-person meetings organized by organizations like the National MS Society. I even got involved in advocacy efforts, which gave me a renewed sense of purpose. However, being a person with MS who lives life with some limitations, some things just do not work as far as what people believe they have given you "access" to. For instance, I have had trouble getting into government office buildings for meetings, and I can imagine that others who needed accommodations did as well.

One time I went to one government building and they had "handicap" access, but you had to go around to the side of the building, and to get to that side of the building, you had to walk up some steps. I don't understand who is supposed to be able to use this or have access to these resources when this is a real situation that people face! If you are in a wheelchair or have mobility challenges, how are you even going to get to the access button to get into the building? They have a wonderful button you can press—if you can get to it—yet in that situation, a person facing certain challenges can't even use it.

To continue to share knowledge and give voice to the needs of people living with limitations, I decided to do more advocacy work. There was an opportunity for me to help with advocacy by writing letters, but I found this process to be, much like everything else, frustrating. My symptoms rendered me unable to write letters due to my cognitive abilities. I was so annoyed because it had been suggested that I could do advocacy work from home. However, to be able to make an impact, you have to reach the right people and people have to get back to you . . . and you also have to be clear in your communication.

On my clear days, I could write letters and follow up with people I had not heard back from yet, but on my unclear days, I could not. In the end, I would be sitting there waiting and waiting and waiting, unable to continue the follow-up efforts. The frustration this caused me would also put me back into a cycle of not being able to effectively manage my overall health. Stress causes flare-ups, and I could not afford that on my journey. So, I had to put a pause on writing letters for advocacy.

My experience, however, did help me better understand the access needs of people living with limitations and mobility challenges and how important support is for these people. Instead of writing letters, I decided to focus on providing support through participating in support groups.

Support groups offered unique experiences based on the participants and their needs. Larger groups like the National MS Society, for example, brought patients from all over the country together through virtual meetings. The ability to be in touch with each other from different places was a Godsend! Technology allowed people who might have otherwise felt isolated to feel connected and share their stories.

Technology played a crucial role in bridging the distance between members, making it possible for me to participate despite not being able to travel in person. These virtual meetings opened doors and facilitated access to vital resources and information.

MS affects millions of people worldwide, and research shows that it impacts individuals from diverse racial backgrounds. Recognizing the need for inclusivity, the MS Society also hosts events and discussions tailored to different kinds of people, including women, men, and specific ethnic communities. It's incredible to see the diversity and support within the MS community.

Since each support group has its own unique dynamics and benefits, it's essential to find the group and method of attendance that works best for you, as every individual has their own needs and goals. The National MS Society, Norton Neuroscience, and the MS Foundation are just a few organizations that offer support groups. Virtual options have been particularly valuable, as they provide convenience and accessibility for individuals who may have transportation limitations or who live far away.

Through these groups, I have met incredible people who offered valuable guidance, from navigating Social Security disability to finding employers who would be willing to hire individuals living with disabilities. Support groups became an essential resource for me, and writing this book made me realize the profound impact they have had on my life. For me, being a part of these groups offered camaraderie, wisdom, and an opportunity to help others on their journeys.

Support groups became my lifeline during my MS journey, and I am incredibly grateful for the strength and encouragement they provided me. Through these groups, I learned the power of community and the importance of never facing life's challenges alone. With newfound knowledge, resilience, and the support of my peers, I was better equipped to tackle each step of my journey with hope and renewed determination. No matter the format, what matters most is finding a community where you feel understood, supported, and empowered. Together, we can navigate the challenges of MS and find strength in our unified efforts.

# *Chapter 7 - Where I Am Now*

Eventually, other people began to see my progress. My sister told me that she could see I had shifted from mourning my diagnosis to doing what I was able to do in the moment. Living with MS is a continual process of being and learning, as you never know how it will affect you on a particular day. You just have to take it one day at a time.

Having MS has been my biggest challenge in life, and being able to work with the unexpected on a daily basis has been the biggest lesson I have learned. In life in general, we never know how things will pan out. We can plan—or at least try to plan. As I say, "We make plans, and God laughs."

God knows who we are and what we need, and things shift on an ongoing basis. Nothing in life is constant. We will have good days and bad days. We will be impacted by the shifts and changes we face. What we once thought would be may no longer be the next moment. Our goal needs to be the focus on what we are doing every day, how we are impacting other people's lives, and how we are living to our fullest potential. It's important to continue to improve your well-being and your thought process about life and what you face.

I have a miracle friend[4] who I often talk to about my journey, and I even shared details with her about writing

_______________

[4] A miracle friend is a volunteer role to meet with people who are unhoused. There is a specific program that allows people to request

this book. She mentioned that she was deeply impressed by what I was trying to do. I know what I am here for. I know I am here to live my life in the best way possible and to encourage other people along their journeys as well. This is what I get to do and how I get to show up daily, even on the days when I don't feel like getting out of bed.

For me, to be able to step into my next phase of life, encourage others, and be an example, I need to continually work to improve my well-being and my thought process. We can do better when we are better. We can feel better when we are better. This is how I am moving forward as I go along my journey. This is how I am showing up daily in taking care of myself and doing what is necessary to take better care of my health and my person and, as the kids say, "live your best life." I am here to live my life to the fullest and to inspire others on their journeys as well. This is where I am now.

---

a "friend" to talk to. This program partners volunteers with unhoused people who may face loneliness.

# References of Studies Mentioned in Ms. Pettus' Bio

"Prevalence of MS More Than Doubles Estimate." *National Multiple Sclerosis Society.*
https://www.nationalmssociety.org/About-the-Society/MS-Prevalence.

Langer-Gould, Annette M. MD, PhD, Edlin Grisell Gonzales MA, Jessica B. Smith MPH,  Bonnie H. Li MS, and Lorene M. Nelson PhD, MS. "Racial and Ethnic Disparities in Multiple Sclerosis Prevalence." *Neurology* 98, no. 18 (2022).
https://doi.org/10.1212/WNL.0000000000200151.

Wahls, Terry L., and Eve Adamson. 2014. *The Wahls Protocol: A Radical New Way to Treat  All Chronic Autoimmune Conditions Using Paleo Principles*. Penguin Group USA.

Stuifbergen, Alexa, PhD, RN, FAAN, Heather Becker, PhD, Carolyn Phillips, PhD, RN, FAAN, Shalonda Horton, PhD, RN, Janet Morrison, PhD, RN, MSCN, and Francisco Perez, PhD. 2020. "The Experience of African-American Women with Multiple Sclerosis." *International Journal of MS Care* 23, no. 2 (2021). https://doi.org/10.7224/1537-2073.2019-068.

**Resources**

**Support Groups**

Norton Neuroscience - https://nortonhealthcare.com/services-and-conditions/neurosciences/patient-resources/multiple-sclerosis-support

National MS Society - https://www.nationalmssociety.org/Resources-Support

Multiple Sclerosis Foundation - https://msfocus.org/Get-Help/Support-Groups

**Online Multiple Sclerosis Support Groups**

Healthline: Living with Multiple Sclerosis - https://www.healthline.com/multiple-sclerosis/living-with-ms

Healthline's MS Buddy - https://apps.apple.com/us/app/bezzy-ms-multiple-sclerosis/id1040195462

MS World - https://www.msworld.org/

Multiple Sclerosis Foundation Facebook Group - https://www.facebook.com/groups/msfocus

Multiple Sclerosis Association of America (MSAA) Online Support Forum - https://mymsaa.org/msaa-community/my-msaa-community-forum

**Workout Support**

MS Gym- www.exercisewithms.com

**Organization**

Todoist - https://get.todoist.io/76a5msjc54fn

## About *My Journey with MS: A Story of Change, Hope, Faith, and Resilience*

*My Journey with MS: A Story of Change, Hope, Faith, and Resilience* is a heartfelt and empowering short narrative story that chronicles one woman's transformative experience living with multiple sclerosis (MS). Through the candid and engaging narrative of Kim's experiences, readers embark on a journey of profound understanding and self-discovery. Kim navigates the challenges and uncertainties of MS with hope, fortified by her deep faith and unbreakable resilience. Her story is a testament to the power of community, as she finds strength in support groups and connects with fellow individuals facing similar trials. With authenticity and grace, Kim shares the highs and lows of her battles, the unwavering support of her loved ones, and the importance of adapting to life's unexpected twists. This book serves as a beacon of inspiration to anyone confronting adversity, reminding us that embracing change, holding on to hope, and nurturing our faith can lead to transformative growth and a life defined by resilience.

## About Kimberly Pettus

In 2019, the National Multiple Sclerosis (MS) Society reported that one million people in the United States are living with MS. This figure is important, as statistics impact how funds and research are allocated. In addition, studies show that African American women are often misdiagnosed and receive inadequate healthcare.

This is my story. I am an African American woman thriving with MS. I speak and write about the time I learned about my diagnosis and how I reimagined and activated who I could become. Throughout my journey, I have learned quite a bit, and now I am sharing more of what I've learned while teaching others how to reimagine their lives and activate who they can become.

I am also a financial process expert and have worked as a senior financial analyst and adjunct professor in finance and accounting. I completed a BA in accounting and finance from The Ohio State University and an MBA in business management from Creighton University.